Sara Swan Miller

"Seahorses, Pipefishes, and Their Kin"

Franklin Watts - A Division of Scholastic Inc.
New York • Toronto • London • Auckland • Sydney
Mexico City • New Delhi • Hong Kong
Danbury, Connecticut

Photographs © 2002: Aaron Norman: 5 top left; American Fisheries Society/Don Flescher: 21; Animals Animals: 17 (Marian Bacon), 5 bottom right (Gregory Brown), 32, 33 (A. Kuiter/OSF), 1 (James Watt); Bruce Coleman Inc.: 7, 13, 43 bottom right (Jane Burton), 39 (Dwight R. Kuhn), 19 (R.L. Sefton); Corbis Images/Barnabas Bosshart: 43 bottom left; Dembinsky Photo Assoc./Mark J. Thomas: 6; Network Aspen/Jones & Shimlock: 37; Peter Arnold Inc.: cover (Yvette Tavernier/Bios), 29 (Norbert Wu); Photo Researchers, NY: 15, 25 (Gregory G. Dimijian), 5 bottom left (Fred McConnaughey), 22, 23 (Mark Smith), 35 (Paul A. Zahl); Visuals Unlimited: 5 top right (Patrice Ceisel), 26, 27 (Dave B. Fleetham), 31 (Edward Lires/John G. Shedd Aquarium), 41 (Gary Meszaros), 43 top (Kjell B. Sandved).

Illustrations by Pedro Julio Gonzalez, Steve Savage, and A. Natacha Pimentel C.

The photo on the cover shows a yellow seahorse. The photo on the title page shows a pygmy seahorse.

Library of Congress Cataloging-in-Publication Data

Miller, Sara Swan.
    Seahorses, pipefishes, and their kin / by Sara Swan Miller; [Pedro Julio Gonzalez, Steve Savage, and A. Natacha Pimentel C., illustrators].
      p. cm. – (animals in order series)
    Includes bibliographical references and index.
    Summary: Describes the common characteristics of the many different-looking fish in the gasterosteiformes order, which includes seahorses, sticklebacks, and the other "bony-bellies."
    ISBN 0-531-12171-2 (lib. bdg.)   0-531-16379-2 (pbk.)
     1. Gasterosteiformes—Juvenile literature. [1. Gasterosteiformes.] I. Gonzalez, Pedro Julio, ill. II. Savage, Steve, ill. III. Pimentel C., A. Natacha, ill. IV. Title. V. Animals in order.
QL637.9.G37 M55 2002
597'.67—dc21   2001003034

Contents

Meet the Seahorses and Their Kin - 4
Traits of Seahorses and Their Kin - 6
The Order of Living Things - 8
How the "Bony-Bellies" Fit In - 10

BONY-BELLIES IN THE ATLANTIC OCEAN
Lined Seahorse - 12
Dwarf Seahorse - 14
Bluespotted Cornetfish - 16
Trumpetfish - 18
Longspine Snipefish - 20

BONY-BELLIES IN THE PACIFIC OCEAN
Tubesnout - 22
Pot-Bellied Seahorse - 24

BONY-BELLIES IN THE INDO-PACIFIC OCEANS
Striped Shrimpfish - 26
Seamoth - 28
Banded Pipefish - 30
Weedy Seadragon - 32
Leafy Seadragon - 34
Harlequin Ghost Pipefish - 36

BONY-BELLIES IN FRESH WATER
Three-Spined Stickleback - 38
Brook Stickleback - 40

Seahorses and Their Kin In Danger - 42
Words to Know - 44
Learning More - 46
Index - 47

Meet the Seahorses and Their Kin

Have you ever seen a seahorse? These peculiar animals don't look like fish at all. They have the head of a horse, the eyes of a chameleon, the snout of an aardvark, and the tail of a monkey. Even stranger, they swim upright!

Seahorses have a close relative—the stickleback. This fish doesn't look at all like a seahorse, though. It looks like other fishes, except for the free-standing spines sticking up on its back. It swims horizontally, as other fishes do.

It's hard to understand why scientists put both of these kinds of fishes in the same group, or *order,* just by looking at them. The order to which both seahorses and sticklebacks belong is called *Gasterosteiformes* (GAS-tare-AH-stay-FORMS), which means "like a stickleback." There are several other fishes in this order, including pipefishes, snipefish, shrimpfish, seamoths, and tubesnouts. None of them looks much like the stickleback. These different fishes don't even look like each other.

On the next page are pictures of four fish from the order Gasterosteiformes. What could they possibly have in common?

Erect seahorse

Brook stickleback

Seamoth

Striped shrimpfish

Traits of Seahorses and Their Kin

One thing almost all of these fishes share is a long, tubular snout and a very small mouth. Except for the sticklebacks, most of them do not have teeth. They use their snouts to suck up their food.

Beyond that, it's hard to see anything else that these fishes have in common. If you understand what the scientific name for the sticklebacks means, however, you will begin to understand why these fishes are in the same order. The sticklebacks are called Gasterosteidae. Gaster is the Greek word for belly, and osteus is the Greek word for bone. Sticklebacks have bony plates on their bellies and no true scales. Most of the other fishes in this order also lack scales and have bony rings or plates on their bodies instead.

What accounts for the fact that these fishes look so different? Scientists believe that all "bony-bellies"

Most gasterosteiformes have long snouts and small mouths.

6

have a common *ancestor* that looked a lot like a stickleback. As millions of years went by, new *species* evolved with shapes and habits that suited their lifestyles. This idea is known as *divergent evolution*. Each species diverged, or became different from the common ancestor.

Scientists notice a few more things that the bony-bellies have in common. They have soft fin rays and *pelvic fins* on their abdomens. Looking inside, scientists see that their air bladders don't have ducts or tubes connecting them to the gut, as other fishes do, and that they have very primitive kidneys.

One last thing that these fishes have in common is that many of them care for their young before they hatch. Seahorses and pipefishes carry their eggs in pouches on their bellies. Sticklebacks build nests for their young and fight off any strange fishes that try to eat them. But other fishes in this order, including the snipefish and seamoths, just lay their eggs and swim away.

A male pipefish carries eggs on his belly.

The Order of Living Things

A tiger has more in common with a house cat than with a daisy. A true bug is more like a butterfly than a jellyfish. Scientists arrange living things into groups based on how they look and how they act. A tiger and a house cat belong to the same group, but a daisy belongs to a different group.

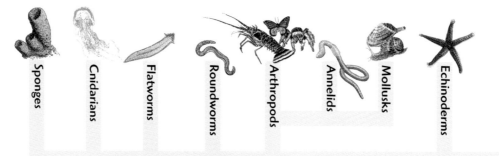

Sponges · Cnidarians · Flatworms · Roundworms · Arthropods · Annelids · Mollusks · Echinoderms

Animals

Plants · Fungi · Protists · Monerans

All living things can be placed in one of five groups called *kingdoms*: the plant kingdom, the animal kingdom, the fungus kingdom, the moneran kingdom, or the protist kingdom. You can probably name many of the creatures in the plant and animal kingdoms. The fungus kingdom includes mushrooms, yeasts, and molds. The moneran and protist kingdoms contain thousands of living things that are too small to see without a microscope.

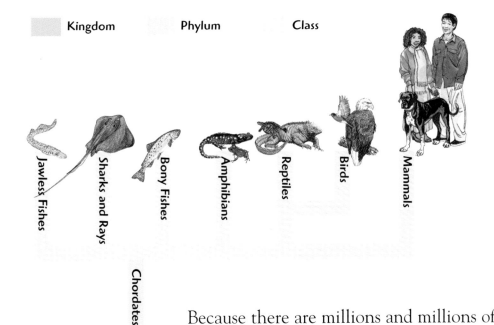

Kingdom Phylum Class

Jawless Fishes

Sharks and Rays

Bony Fishes

Amphibians

Reptiles

Birds

Mammals

Chordates

Because there are millions and millions of living things on Earth, some of the members of one kingdom may not seem all that similar. The animal kingdom includes creatures as different as tarantulas and trout, jellyfish and jaguars, salamanders and sparrows, elephants and earthworms.

To show that an elephant is more like a jaguar than an earthworm, scientists further separate the creatures in each kingdom into more specific groups. The animal kingdom is divided into nine *phyla.* Humans belong to the chordate phylum. All chordates have a backbone.

Each phylum can be subdivided into many *classes.* Humans, mice, and elephants all belong to the mammal class. Each class is divided into *orders;* orders are divided into *families,* families into *genera,* and genera into *species.* All the members of a species are very similar and can mate and produce healthy young.

9

How the "Bony-Bellies" Fit In

You can probably guess that the bony-bellies belong to the animal kingdom. They have much more in common with spiders and snakes than they do with maple trees and morning glories.

Bony-bellies are members of the chordate phylum. Almost all chordates have a backbone and a skeleton. Can you think of other chordates? Examples include elephants, mice, snakes, frogs, fishes, whales, and humans.

Fishes belong to one of seven classes. There are about fifty-nine orders of fishes. The bony-bellies make up one of these orders.

Scientists divide bony-bellies into eleven families and seventy-four genera. There are 275 species. Bony-bellies live in oceans, usually in coastal waters, around the world, and a few live in fresh-water ponds and streams. Let's find out more about these peculiar fishes!

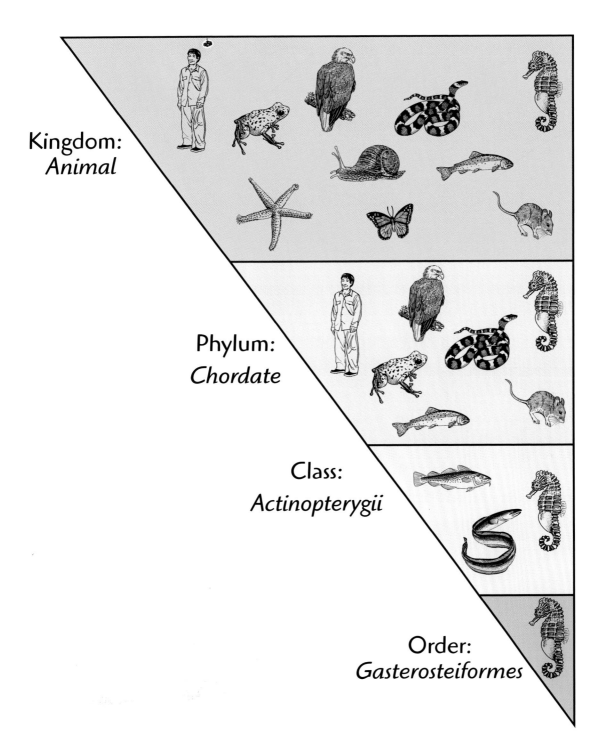

Kingdom: *Animal*

Phylum: *Chordate*

Class: *Actinopterygii*

Order: *Gasterosteiformes*

Seahorses

FAMILY: Syngnathidae
COMMON EXAMPLE: Lined seahorse
GENUS AND SPECIES: *Hippocampus erectus*
SIZE: 8 inches (20 cm)

A male lined seahorse clings to a seaweed stem, bending back and forth. He has been carrying his *mate's* eggs in his pouch for weeks. Now he is in labor. You can see the muscle spasms in his stomach. Suddenly, the baby seahorses begin shooting out of his pouch. He keeps bending, and babies keep shooting out. The babies—nearly two hundred of them—swim off on their own. They will have to fend for themselves. The tired father rests quietly in the seaweed.

Like other seahorses, lined seahorses mate for life. When the moon is full, a male approaches his mate and begins courting her. For several days he entices her with color changes and by quivering his body. Finally, the two begin swimming along with each other and it's time to mate. The female deposits her pinkish eggs into her mate's *brood* pouch, where he fertilizes them. He will protect them inside the pouch until they hatch.

These seahorses are well *camouflaged* and blend in with their surroundings. They cling to seaweed or coral with their gripping tails and rest upright. They can change color to match whatever they are hiding in. As long as the seahorses stay still, hungry fishes, birds, sea turtles, or crabs don't know that food is lurking in front of them.

Seahorses

FAMILY: Syngnathidae
COMMON EXAMPLE: Dwarf seahorse
GENUS AND SPECIES: *Hippocampus zosterae*
SIZE: 1 inch (2.5 cm)

It's not hard to figure out how the dwarf seahorse got its name. It is tiny—no bigger than the tip of your thumb. It lives among seaweeds and coral in warm oceans off the coasts of Bermuda and the Bahamas, and in the Gulf of Mexico. Like other seahorses, it can change color to blend in with its surroundings.

It's a good thing that dwarf seahorses are so well camouflaged because there are plenty of fishes, crustaceans, and even sea anemones that enjoy a seahorse meal. When a seahorse ventures out from its hiding place, it's a slow swimmer. It swims about by fluttering its transparent *dorsal fin*, with a little help from its *pectoral fins*, and it's easy for *predators* to catch. Its upright position may help it hide in the seaweed, but because its body isn't horizontal and stream-lined, a seahorse can't zip about like other fishes.

What do these little seahorses find to eat with their small mouths? Pygmy seahorses use their snouts like straws to suck up tiny animals such as brine shrimp. But seahorses have no stomachs. The food goes from the mouth to the intestine. Since they can't store food in their stomachs, seahorses have to eat constantly. If they are deprived of food for even a short time, they will die.

Cornetfishes

FAMILY: Fistulariidae
COMMON EXAMPLE: Bluespotted cornetfish
GENUS AND SPECIES: *Fistularia tabacaria*
SIZE: 4 to 6 feet (1.2 to 1.8 m)

A cornetfish doesn't look at all like a seahorse, but it certainly does look strange. Its incredibly long, slim body looks like a cornet, which is a trumpet-like, brass instrument. Its snout is so long that it looks as if the fish is *all* snout. Some people call it a "flutemouth." From the end of its tail floats a very long *filament* that is almost as long as its body. The filament is lined with sensory pores, which may help the cornetfish sense *prey* or predators lurking behind it. Like many other bony-bellies, the cornetfish has no scales, and some species have hard plates embedded in their skin.

Compared with the rest of its body, a cornetfish's mouth is small. But it's big enough for the cornetfish to catch and eat smaller fishes. It lurks around reefs and wrecked ships on the ocean floor, as deep as 600 feet (200 m), waiting for schools of little fish to swim by. Then it whips out and ambushes them. At night, it swims about over the open sand, ready to snatch other passing fish. Sometimes it sucks up small invertebrates or little crabs.

Cornetfishes are solitary creatures, never swimming in schools like many other kinds of fishes. They don't need the safety of a school because they are protected by their large size and their camouflage.

Their brownish bodies, speckled with light blue spots, help them blend in with corals and seaweeds where they hide.

Cornetfishes can be found almost anywhere off the Atlantic coastline and in the Pacific and Indian Oceans. Some live off the coast of Africa and others can be found off the coast of Canada, all the way down to Brazil.

Trumpetfishes

FAMILY: Aulostomidae
COMMON EXAMPLE: Trumpetfish
GENUS AND SPECIES: *Aulostomus maculatus*
SIZE: 2 to 3 feet (35 to 91 cm)

A large, spotted trumpetfish lurks behind an outcropping of coral, waiting in *ambush* for a small fish to happen by. Finally, it spots a school of little fish swimming closer and closer. The trumpetfish zips out of its hiding place, opens its trumpet-like mouth, and slurps up the first fish it can catch.

Sometimes trumpetfish use another method to ambush prey. They swim behind the bodies of larger, *herbivorous* fishes. Their unsuspecting prey isn't afraid of the herbivorous fish and doesn't notice the trumpetfish hiding behind it. This allows the trumpetfishes to get very close to their prey before attacking them.

Trumpetfishes are predators, but they are also prey. They are timid, always on the alert. If they spot a bigger fish or even a diver, they swim away in a horizontal position, pushing their stiff bodies along with their tiny fins. But if a trumpetfish feels cornered, it has a different trick. It zips among some vertical coral or weeds and turns head-down to hide. Its long, thin body makes for good camouflage, and pale lines and small black spots on its sides help it blend in with the coral and weeds. Like many other bony-bellies, a trumpetfish can also change color to blend in with its surroundings.

Look at the picture of the cornetfish and compare it to the trumpetfish. Both look very similar, with their long, slim bodies and tube-shaped mouths. But you can tell them apart. A trumpetfish is flattened sideways and has small spines on its back. A cornetfish is flattened from top to bottom and trails a long filament behind it.

Snipefish

FAMILY: Centriscidae
COMMON EXAMPLE: Longspine snipefish
GENUS AND SPECIES: *Macroramphosus scolopax*
SIZE: 7 inches (20 cm)

How did the longspine snipefish get its name? It's snout reminds people of the beak of a snipe, a bird with an unusually large bill. This particular snipefish has several spines on its back.

Most bony-bellies live in shallow waters and hide among seaweeds. Snipefishes, however, prefer to live in the deep waters of the open ocean. Most longspine snipefish live off the North American and South American coasts. Other species of snipefishes live in the Indo-Pacific oceans, and some live off the coasts of Hawaii and California. As long as the water is fairly warm, snipefishes will live there. They use their long snout to vacuum up tiny plants and animals.

Living in the open ocean without seaweed and coral to hide in is dangerous. How do snipefish protect themselves from predators? One way is to travel in schools. Snipefish usually form schools of hundreds of individuals. When a predator attacks, it may be able to catch a few, but most will get away. There is safety in numbers!

A snipefish has other ways to protect itself, too. Those spines on its back discourage any predator that thinks about biting into it. Even more important, snipefish are excellent swimmers, and they can swim backward as easily as they swim forward.

Tubesnouts

FAMILY: Aulorhynchidae
COMMON EXAMPLE: Tubesnout
GENUS AND SPECIES: *Aulorhynchus flavidus*
SIZE: 7 inches (18 cm)

You don't have to think hard to see how the tubesnout got its name. It uses its long tube to suck up tiny creatures floating in the water, including shrimp, tiny fish larvae, and fish eggs.

Of all the bony-bellies, tubesnouts look most like sticklebacks, the fish for which the order is named. They have spines on their backs, like sticklebacks, but their bodies are longer and are covered in armor.

If you find yourself on a dock overlooking a bay, look down into the water. You may see a large school of tubesnouts swimming in the shallow water. Try to spot some with black-and-white snouts and bright-red gills. Those are the males flaunting their breeding-season colors.

Male tubesnouts don't protect their eggs in pouches, as seahorses do, but they do defend their young. A male builds a nest among giant kelp fronds and glues it all together with a sticky substance that he makes in his kidneys. As a female lays her eggs in the nest and the

22

male fertilizes them, the eggs stick to the gluey nest. The male defends the nest fiercely against all enemies. He even drives away other tubesnouts, because even they may eat the eggs.

There are only two species of tubesnouts. The larger, *Aulorhynchus flavidus*, is found in the Pacific Ocean along the North American coast, from Alaska to Baja. The other, *Aulichthys japonicus*, lives in the western Pacific Ocean, off the coast of Japan.

Seahorses

FAMILY: Syngnathidae
COMMON EXAMPLE: Pot-bellied seahorse
GENUS AND SPECIES: *Hippocampus abdominalis*
SIZE: 10 inches (25 cm)

Male seahorses grow big bellies when they are incubating their eggs, but both male and female pot-bellied seahorses *always* look pregnant. When a male is pregnant, his belly grows even bigger.

Pot-bellied seahorses produce several broods over the summer. The male incubates the eggs for four weeks before the tiny young burst from his pouch. They rise quickly to the surface of the water and cling with their tails to floating debris. These seahorses have so many young each year that you would think they would overrun the ocean. But there are plenty of fishes and other predators that slurp up the little seahorse babies hiding in the weeds.

Like many other seahorses, pot-bellies have knobs and spines on their heads. These are called *cirri* (SEE-ree), and the pot-bellies have especially long ones. Their cirri help camouflage the seahorses among the seaweed. The cirri may also help protect the seahorses from predators. Who wants a mouthful of spines? A seahorse's armor of bony rings helps protect it too.

A seahorse has another way of protecting itself. When it is scared, it curls its tail around its snout and makes itself into a small ball. That makes it even harder for predators to see it!

Pot-bellied seahorses live in the shallow waters around Australia and New Zealand, but they are becoming rare. This is partially because people catch and dry them and sell them as medicine.

Shrimpfish

FAMILY: Centriscidae
COMMON EXAMPLE: Striped shrimpfish
GENUS AND SPECIES: *Aeoliscus strigatus*
SIZE: 6 inches (14 cm)

If you see a school of shrimpfish in a bed of seagrass, at first you might think they've lost their minds. All of them swim along, snout down and tail up. Is that any way for a fish to behave?

When you think about it, though, you'll realize that swimming vertically is a good adaptation for hiding from predators. Shrimpfish live together in schools among seagrass or staghorn corals. Their long, vertical bodies blend in well with their surroundings. Stripes on their sides help to camouflage them as well.

Some shrimpfish live among the spines of sea urchins, which protects them even better. Many sea urchins have poison in their long, sharp spines. Most predators leave them—and the shrimpfish—alone!

Shrimpfish have another way of protecting themselves. Like many other bony-bellies, they have armored bodies. Instead of scales, they have bony plates under their skin. Because of their armor and their ways of camouflaging themselves, adult shrimpfish are well protected from predators. Young shrimpfish, how-ever, are not so lucky. Many larger fishes prey on these small and delicate creatures.

As they swim about head-down, shrimpfish forage for food. They use their long snouts to vacuum up tiny plants and animals in the water. Like seahorses, shrimpfish have no teeth. They swallow their food whole.

Seamoths

FAMILY: Pegasidae
COMMON EXAMPLE: Seamoth
GENUS AND SPECIES: *Eurypegasus draconis*
SIZE: 3 inches (8 cm)

The seamoth is aptly named. It has big, winglike pectoral fins on each side of its long body, which it uses to "fly" through the water. Some people call seamoths dragonfish because of their winglike fins. But seamoths are small and not at all fierce—hardly like dragons!

Seamoths live on the bottom of shallow, coastal waters. They can actually walk along the seabed using special spines on their pectoral fins. When they rest quietly on the bottom, these flattened fish are hard to spot. Their gray-and-brown-spotted bodies blend in perfectly with the pebbly bottom. Bony rings of armor all down their bodies also help protect these small fish. Their armor is fused on the heads and bodies, which makes them stiff. The tail armor is not fused. They use their flexible tails to help them swim.

Since they don't move about much, seamoths become covered with parasites and algae. So every few days, they shed their skin. They make a sudden, quick jump and their skin slips off in one piece to reveal a new skin beneath.

During mating season, seamoths get together and remain in pairs. They will mate only with each other. But, unlike many other

bony-bellies, they don't take care of their young. The male fertilizes the female's eggs in the water, and the two just swim away.

Seamoths live in shallow waters, from the Indian Ocean to the central Pacific. They can be found along the coast of southern Japan, and all the way down to Australia and Micronesia. One species lives off the coast of Hawaii.

Pipefishes

FAMILY: Syngnathidae
COMMON EXAMPLE: Banded pipefish
GENUS AND SPECIES: *Corythoicthys flavofasiatus*
SIZE: 6 inches (15 cm)

Look at the picture of the banded pipefish and imagine bending it into an s-shape. It would look like a seahorse! Pipefishes and seahorses, in fact, are very closely related and are in the same family. They have a lot in common.

Like seahorses, pipefishes are encased in rings of bony armor, from their necks all the way down to their tails. The armor protects them, but it makes them stiff so they aren't very fast swimmers. Also like seahorses, pipefishes have no fin spines or pelvic fins. They swim about by fluttering their dorsal fins, which act like outboard motors. Unlike seahorses, they sometimes wriggle through the water looking very much like sea snakes.

A banded pipefish is like a seahorse in another way. The male protects eggs and young inside a pouch. He has folds of skin on his belly that can form a brood pouch, where the young are safe until they are fully formed, tiny adults. Even after they shoot out of the pouch, the young may dive back in when danger threatens.

A pipefish's snout is long and tube-shaped like a seahorse's and is formed by bones that are permanently locked together. Like a seahorse, a pipefish sucks up tiny crustaceans and baby fish with its

snout. But pipefishes are picky eaters. If they don't like what they have sucked up, they will blow it back out.

Pipefishes live in warm and temperate oceans all over the world. There are about two hundred species—more than there is in any other family of bony-bellies!

Seadragons

FAMILY: Syngnathidae
COMMON EXAMPLE: Weedy seadragon
GENUS AND SPECIES: *Phyllopteryx taeniolatus*
SIZE: 17 inches (46 cm)

A weedy seadragon is certainly odd looking! It has small, leaf-like things growing out of its body. Most weedy seadragons are red with yellow spots and purple-blue bars. The leaves are usually purple with a black border. A weedy seadragon is well camouflaged. It is perfectly hidden in rocky reefs, seagrass, and seaweed beds in the shallow waters just off the coastline.

If you can get past a seadragon's leaves and look closely at its snout and body, you'll see that it looks a lot like a seahorse. It's shaped like a seahorse, and it's even covered with armor-like plates instead of scales. Like the pipefishes, it is a very close seahorse relative.

Seadragons don't have a brood pouch, unlike seahorses and pipefishes, but the males do protect the eggs. In breeding season, seadragons move into even shallower waters. A female lays up to 250 bright red eggs in a special spot under the male's tail. He fertilizes them and protects them there in little cups. He carries the eggs for as long as eight weeks before they hatch. Then the young have to fend for themselves.

Newly hatched seadragons are small and not as weedy as adults. Their armor isn't as hard, either. As you might suspect, they have a lot of enemies. Anemones, crabs, and hydroids all prey on young seadragons.

Seadragons

FAMILY: Syngnathidae
COMMON EXAMPLE: Leafy seadragon
GENUS AND SPECIES: *Phycodurus eques*
SIZE: 17 1/2 inches (45 cm)

A leafy seadragon is even stranger than a weedy seadragon and even better camouflaged. Its body trails leafy flaps that make it look like a bunch of floating seaweed. Usually, it hangs motionless in the water among kelp forests, where few predators will spot it. When a seadragon needs to get somewhere, it flutters its delicate fins faster than the eye can see and glides gracefully along in the water.

As you might suspect, a leafy seadragon is also closely related to the seahorses and it, too, is covered with similar armor plates. Like the weedy seadragon, the male leafy seadragon protects the eggs inside cups under his tail.

Leafy seadragons are beautiful to watch as they float through the water waving their leafy flaps. But their beauty may become their downfall. Lots of aquarium owners love keeping seadragons, and they buy them from collectors. But leafy seadragons are so popular that collectors have caught and shipped far too many of these rare fish, which live only off the coast of Australia. In 1991 the Australian authorities realized how rare the leafy seadragons were becoming, and they declared them a protected species. But still some unlawful collectors poach seadragons hiding in the seagrass.

Leafy seadragons face other problems. Fertilizer from farms flows as run-off into the shallow waters where the seadragons live and clogs it. Factories also create pollution in the seadragons' watery habitat. Leafy seadragons have been around for millions of years. Will they survive people?

Ghost Pipefishes

FAMILY: Solenostomidae
COMMON EXAMPLE: Harlequin ghost pipefish
GENUS AND SPECIES: *Solenostomus paradoxus*
SIZE: 3 to 5 inches (8 to 13 cm)

The harlequin ghost pipefish is another bony-belly that relies on camouflage for protection. It is covered with spines and is mottled with dark red, yellow, and orange splotches. When it hides among coral reefs, seaweed, or spiny sea urchins, it is almost impossible to spot. The star-shaped plates on its body also help protect it. What fish would want to bite into a spiny, armored ghost pipefish?

Ghost pipefishes, like seahorses and pipefishes, protect their eggs in pouches. But this time it's the female who does the job. She has large pelvic fins that connect to each other and to her body to form a brood pouch. The eggs stick to special cells on the inside of her pelvic fins. When the eggs finally hatch, the young are on their own. A female ghost pipefish may produce as many as 350 eggs at a time. That's a lot of new ghost pipefish coming into the world! But there are so many predators out there, from fish to anemones, that very few of the young survive into adulthood.

Like many bony-bellies, ghost pipefishes are ambush hunters. They lurk in camouflage and suck up small creatures that float by. In the open, they are slow swimmers, getting around by rapidly fanning their fins. But even though they are slow, these fish can position

themselves in exactly the right spot among the corals, where neither predators nor prey will spot them.

There are only three species of ghost pipefishes. All of them live in warm, tropical waters between South Africa and Japan.

Sticklebacks

FAMILY: Gasterosteidae
COMMON EXAMPLE: Three-spined stickleback
GENUS AND SPECIES: *Gasterosteus aculeatus*
SIZE: 4 inches (11 cm)

Spring is mating time for the three-spined stickleback. A male gets busy building his nest. He chooses a spot among the stems of plants where the water flows nicely but not too quickly. Then he nips off bits of other plants and begins gluing them to the plant stems. His kidneys create a sticky fluid that binds it all together.

Once he has built a platform, he scoops up sand from the bottom of the ocean and blows it over the foundation of his nest. Then he begins building up the rest of the nest. Every so often he butts against it, checking to see if it's solid. When he's done, he has created a hollow, rounded nest with an entrance hole on one side and an exit hole on the other. Finally, he does a "plastering" job on the inside of the nest. He goes in and out, turning around and around inside, adding more glue until the walls are smooth.

By this time, the male's belly has turned bright red in order to attract females. When a female comes by, he does a twisting, turning courtship dance to lure her to the nest. Once she has laid her eggs inside the nest and the male has fertilized them, though, he drives her away. He waits outside the nest for another female to come by, and another, and another, until his nest is full of fertilized eggs.

The male guards his nest until the eggs hatch. He fans the eggs with his tail to supply them with oxygen. When other fish come by, he chases them off. He will even drive away the females that laid the eggs! Once they are hatched, though, the young swim off to fend for themselves.

Sticklebacks

FAMILY: Gasterosteidae
COMMON EXAMPLE: Brook stickleback
GENUS AND SPECIES: *Culaea inconstans*
SIZE: 3 1/3 inches (8.7 cm)

Brook sticklebacks are favorites of children and adults alike. These busy, quick fish live in clear brooks, streams, ponds, and lakes in northern North America, where they are easy to watch. Some people even keep them as aquarium pets. But people find that they can't keep other fishes in the same aquariums, because sticklebacks are very fierce and greedy. They attack bigger fishes and bite off pieces of their fins. They devour other fishes' eggs, and even eggs of their own species.

Brook sticklebacks are different from other North American species. Others have bony plates on their scaleless bodies, but you won't see plates on a brook stickleback. Only if you look through a microscope will you see minute, bony plates on its sides. Like other sticklebacks, a brook stickleback has free-standing spines on its back. Usually it has five, but sometimes it has four or six. It uses its spines when it is defending its territory and fighting off other males.

Like other sticklebacks, a male brook stickleback builds a nest that is cemented together with glue. He lures several females inside, one after another, and keeps them there until they lay eggs.

Then he drives them away and guards the nest. Even after the young hatch, he takes care of them. If they swim away, he catches them in his mouth and spits them back into the nest. He only gives up when the young get too fast for him to catch. From then on, they're on their own.

Seahorses and Their Kin In Danger

Over millions of years, seahorses and their kin have become so well adapted to life in the sea that you would think they must be thriving. Sadly, though, many species are threatened or endangered. Some are believed to be on the verge of extinction. Scientists who study seahorses say that there are now only half as many creatures of certain species as there were just seven years ago. What is wrong?

One of the worst threats facing seahorses and pipefishes is that they are used as a popular medicine in Asian countries. People collect them, dry and powder them, and then sell them at very high prices. Just one kilogram of dried seahorse, which amounts to three hundred to four hundred animals, can sell for over $1,200 U.S.! It's no wonder that poor people who are trying to support their families are eager to make money off seahorses and pipefishes. In 1996 alone, twenty million seahorses were caught and sold.

Not all of these seahorses and pipefishes are made into medicine. Many are dried and sold as gifts in souvenir shops. Others are sold as aquarium pets. Seadragons are also caught and sold as pets, but they are very hard to keep and usually die. Many scientists believe that they are becoming more and more rare in their natural *habitat*.

Seahorses and their kin face other dangers as well. As coral reefs and seagrass beds are destroyed, the fish that live there vanish as

well. Pollution in the oceans is also a major problem.

People concerned about saving seahorses are working hard to protect their habitats and fight against the seahorse trade. But it's not an easy task. It would be a tragedy if seahorses and their kin vanished forever.

Dried seahorses are sometimes sold in souvenir shops.

Some seahorses are kept as pets in aquariums.

Seahorses are used in many medicinal products.

Words to Know

ambush—a surprise attack

ancestor—a relative of a person or animal that lived a long time ago

brood—the young of an animal

camouflage—to hide by blending into the surrounding environment

cirri (sing. cirrus)—knobs and spines on a seahorse's head

class—a group of creatures within a phylum that share certain characteristics

divergent evolution—the process by which new species with different characteristics develop from a common ancestor

dorsal fin—a fin on a fish's back

family—a group of creatures within an order that share certain characteristics

filament—a thin, flexible, threadlike object

gasterosteiformes—the order to which seahorses, sticklebacks, and their kin belong

genus (plural genera)—a group of creatures within a family that share certain characteristics

habitat—the place where an organism is best suited to live

herbivorous—feeding on plants

kingdom—one of the five divisions into which all living things are placed: the animal kingdom, the plant kingdom, the fungus kingdom, the moneran kingdom, and the protist kingdom

44

mate—a breeding partner; to breed and produce young

order—a group of creatures within a class that shares certain characteristics

pectoral fin—one of a pair of fins on a fish's side toward the front of its body

pelvic fin—one of a pair of fins on a fish's side toward the back of its belly

phylum (plural **phyla**)—a group of creatures within a kingdom that shares certain characteristics

predator—an animal that hunts and eats other animals

prey—an animal hunted for food by another animal (a predator)

species—a group of creatures within a genus that shares certain characteristics. Members of a species can mate and produce young.

Learning More

Books

Bailey, Jill. *How Fish Swim (Nature's Mysteries)*. Tarrytown: Benchmark Books, 1997.

Blum, Mark. *Beneath the Sea in 3-D*. San Francisco: Chronicle Books, 1997.

Miller, Sara Swan. *Funny Fishes*. Danbury, CT: Franklin Watts, 2001.

Parker, Steve. *Eyewitness: Fish*. New York: DK Publishing, 2000.

Stefoff, Rebecca. *Sea Horse*. Tarrytown: Benchmark Books, 1997.

Zim, Herbert S. *Fishes: A Guide to Fresh- and Salt-Water Species*. New York: St. Martin's Press, 2001.

Web Sites

Kingdom of the Seahorse
http://www.pbs.org/wgbh/nova/seahorse
Offers seahorse basics and an account of seahorse dads.

Seahorse Park
http://www.poost.nl/seahorse/index.html
Features seahorse news, a seahorse gallery, facts and figures, and links to other seahorse sites.

Page on Seahorses
http://www.geocities.com/RainForest/Canopy/7897/page2.html
Find general information on seahorses, descriptions of several species, and links to other seahorse sites.

Index

Babies, 7, 12, 24, 27, 29, 30, 33, 36,
    39, 41
Banded pipefish, 30–31, *31*
Belly, 6, *7*, 7, 24, 38
Bluespotted cornetfish, 16–17, *17*
Bony-bellies, 6, 7, 10, 16, 18, 20, 22,
    26, 29, 31, 36
Brood pouch, 7, 12, 22, 24, 30, 32, 36
Brook stickleback, 5, 40–41, *41*
Camouflage, 12, 14, 16, 18, 24, 26,
    32, 34, 36
Cornetfish, 16–17, *17*, 19
Dwarf seahorse, 14–15, *15*
Eggs, *7*, 7, 12, 22, 22–23, 24, 29, 30,
    32, 33, 34, 36, 38, 39, 40
Endangered species, 25, 34, 42
Fins, 7, 14, 18, 28, 30, 34, 36
Food, 6, 14, 16, 18, 27, 31
Gasterosteiformes, 4, 6, 11
Ghost pipefish, 36–37, *37*
Harlequin ghost pipefish, 36–37, *37*
Kidney, 7, 22, 38
Leafy seadragon, 34–35, *35*
Lined seahorse, 12–13, *13*
Longspine snipefish, 20–21, *21*
Mating, 12, 28, 38
Mouth, 6, 6, 14, 16, 19

Nest, 7, 22, 23, 38, 39, 40, 41
Pipefish, 4, *7*, 7, 30–31, *31*, 32, 36, 42
Pollution, 35, 43
Pot-bellied seahorse, 24–25, *25*
Predator, 7, 14, 16, 18, 20, 24, 26, 27,
    33, 34, 36, 37
Scales, 6, 16, 26, 32
Seadragon, 32–35, *33*, *35*, 42
Seahorse, 5, 7, 12–15, *13*, *15*, 22, 24–
    25, *25*, 27, 30, 32, 34, 36, 42, *43*
Seamoth, 4, 5, 7, 28–29, *29*
Shrimpfish, 4, *5*, 26–27, *27*
Snipefish, 4, 7, 20–21, *21*
Snout, 6, *6*, 14, 16, 20, 24, 26, 27, 30,
    31, 32
Spines, 4, 19, 20, 22, 24, 26, 28, 30,
    36, 40
Stickleback, 4, *5*, 6, 7, 22, 38–41, 39,
    41
Striped shrimpfish, 5, 26–27, *27*
Swimming, 4, 14, 16, 20, 26, 27, 28,
    30, 36
Tail, 12, 16, 24, 26, 28, 30, 33, 34, 39
Three-spined stickleback, 38–39, *39*
Trumpetfish, 18–19, *19*
Tubesnout, 4, 22–23, *23*
Weedy seadragon, 32–33, *33*, 34

About the Author

Sara Swan Miller has enjoyed working with children all her life, first as a Montessori nursery-school teacher and later as an outdoor environmental educator at the Mohonk Preserve in New Paltz, NY. As director of the preserve school program, Miller has led hundreds of school children on field trips and taught them the importance of appreciating and respecting the natural world.

Miller has written a number of children's books, including *Three Stories You Can Read to Your Dog; Three Stories You Can Read to Your Cat; Three More Stories You Can Read to Your Dog; What's in the Woods? An Outdoor Activity Book; Oh, Cats of Camp Rabbitbone; Piggy in the Parlor and Other Tales; Better Than TV;* and *Will You Sting Me? Will You Bite? The Truth About Some Scary-Looking Insects.* She has also written several books on farm animals for the Children's Press True Books series, a set of books on strange fishes, amphibians, reptiles, birds, and mammals for the Watts Library, and several other books in the Animals in Order series.